STOCK TRUCKS

OFF TO THE RACES

PETER & NILDA SESSLER

The Rourke Press, Inc.
Vero Beach, Florida 32964

1218763

PHOTO CREDITS
© ARCA: page 4; © Chevrolet: cover, pages 6, 9, 10, 16, 18, 19, 21, 22; © Chrysler Corporation: page 7; © Flemington Raceway: page 12; © Peter Sessler: pages 13, 15

EDITORIAL SERVICES:
Susan Albury

Library of Congress Cataloging-in-Publication Data

Sessler, Peter C., 1950-
    Stock trucks / Peter Sessler, Nilda Sessler.
        p. cm. — (Off to the races)
    Includes index.
    Summary: Describes NASCAR pick-up truck racing, its rules, how the trucks are equipped, and how fast they travel.
    ISBN 1-57103-285-1
    1. Truck racing Juvenile literature. 2. Stock cars (Automobiles) Juvenile literature.
[1. Truck racing. 2. Stock cars (Automobiles)] I. Sessler, Nilda, 1951- . II. Title. III. Series: Sessler, Peter C., 1950- Off to the races.
GV1034.996.S47 1999
796.72—dc21   99-13827
                                                                        CIP

Printed in the USA

◼◻◻ TABLE OF CONTENTS

■■ PICKUP TRUCKS HIT THE TRACKS!

For the past twenty years, some of the most popular cars sold in the USA weren't cars at all: they were trucks! That included vans and SUVs (sport utility vehicles) but most of all, it was the good old pickup truck.

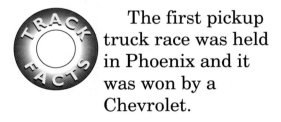 The first pickup truck race was held in Phoenix and it was won by a Chevrolet.

Mini pickup truck racing started in 1998.

In 1994 some people thought that it might be a good idea to have pickup trucks race just like the stock cars. That year there were a few show races at various NASCAR (National Association for Stock Car Racing) stock car races. They were there to see what the **spectators** (SPEK tay torz) thought about them.

Full-size pickup truck racing started in 1995. It has become very popular because the racing is so exciting.

The Craftsman Company sponsored the NASCAR pickup truck series, which is why all trucks that race in the series have Craftsman on the windshield. This is a Dodge Ram.

People liked the idea so much that in 1995, pickup trucks were allowed to race at tracks all over the country. These were full-size trucks. In 1998, there were several show races for the smaller mini pickup trucks, such as the Ford Ranger and Chevrolet S-10.

RACING RULES

The first big racing series for pickup trucks was the Craftsman Series. Craftsman Tools **sponsored** (SPON sird) the series and the races were held on National Association for Stock Car Racing (NASCAR) race tracks.

The safety rules of NASCAR and ARCA (Automobile Racing Club of America) are very important. All drivers must wear a special fireproof suit and helmet. You can also see the heavy steel tubing inside the truck that protects the driver.

NASCAR makes the rules for all the racers to follow for many reasons. First, it is important the trucks be as safe as possible, and secondly, that no one racer has an unfair advantage over other racers. By making all the cars as equal as possible, racing is more fun to watch. That way, the better drivers can win.

Besides NASCAR, there are other groups who have truck races. The Professional Association of Racing Trucks (PARTS) and the Automobile Racing Club of America (ARCA) also have truck racing all over the country.

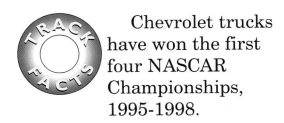

Chevrolet trucks have won the first four NASCAR Championships, 1995-1998.

The rules require that two steel straps be used to hold the windshield in place. The steel tubing or roll cage that protects the driver can be seen here.

◪ CIRCLE TRACK RACING

Pickup trucks race on oval tracks just like the stock cars. Some of them are shaped like the letter D, such as the track in Richmond, Virginia, others are tri-ovals (named after three banked turns), like the track in Daytona, Florida, and still others have four corners, like the track at Indianapolis, Indiana. These tracks are sometimes called circle tracks even though they aren't shaped like circles at all.

Trucks are raced on both short and long tracks. This is a short 5/8 mile long square oval in Flemington, NJ.

To make racing safer, many tracks now use large blocks of fiber-foam on the walls to soak up the force of a crash.

Most of these are paved tracks but races are also held on dirt tracks. The surface on these tracks is made of packed-down clay. The trucks slip and slide so it takes a lot of driving skill to do well.

◼◻◻ THE PICK'EM-UPS

The most popular racing trucks are the Chevrolet C-1500, the Ford F-150, and the Dodge Ram 1500. Unlike the trucks you see on the road, all stock pickup truck racers are two-wheel drive and not four-wheel drive.

Even though the trucks look like the ones you can get at the local car dealer, they do not use the same bodies. If you look closely, you'll see that the front grilles and hoods are flatter and shorter. The pickup bed is also covered because it looks better and helps makes the trucks more stable at high speeds. Trucks raced under PARTS have bodies made of fiberglass or PVC (polyvinyl chloride), a rubber-type material.

Underneath the truck body, pickup trucks have a special tube steel frame which is almost the same as the ones used on the fastest stock cars. The engines are also the same but not quite as powerful.

Racing pickup trucks only look like the ones you can buy at the local dealer. Underneath the body, they are completely different.

◼️◻️ LET'S GO TRUCKIN'!

Racing can be very difficult and it can take a lot of work to get a pickup truck to run perfectly. For this reason, the racers usually arrive at the racetrack a few days before the race. This gives the mechanics time to fix anything that needs to be worked on and to make changes so the truck will run better.

The racing pickups use the same engines and frames as the NASCAR stock cars. However, they aren't as fast because the truck body is not as low and sleek.

It is also important to get to the track early so the driver can take practice laps on the track. Many of the tracks look the same but they have bumps or the banked turns might be higher or lower than the drivers are used to.

This is the view from behind the pace car as the trucks rumble along on the warm-up laps.

Rush, rush, rush! The quicker the truck gets out of the pits, the quicker it can return to the race.

To decide the starting position for each truck, the drivers take their trucks for several **qualifying laps** (KWA la fi ing laps). The fastest truck starts at the inside of the front row in what is called the "pole" position.

On race day, the trucks are slowly led around the track by a **pace car** (PACE kar) to warm up their engines and tires. When the track officials see that everything is okay, the pace car pulls off the track, and the green flag is waved.

All at once the trucks *floor* their gas pedals and the race is on! On the long races, the trucks have to make pit stops to get more gas and change tires because racing tires wear out very quickly.

Finally, the winner takes the checkered flag and the race is over. After the race, the teams pack up all their equipment and travel to the next track.

At the end of the year, the driver who has won the most races becomes champion.

 Pickup trucks have over 650 horsepower and can hit speeds of 160 mph.

During the first three years of NASCAR pickup truck racing, all the trucks came into the pits at the same time, at the halfway mark, for five minutes. The race was then restarted.

◧ GLOSSARY

pace car (PACE kar) — an automobile that leads the field of race cars through a pace lap but does not participate in the race

qualifying laps (KWA la fi ing laps) — laps before a race to see if cars are ready to be in the race

spectators (SPEK tay torz) — people who watch

sponsored (SPON sird) — to be supported financially by a company that then gets to place their advertising on the drivers and the cars

CONVERSION TABLE

5/8 mile ....1 kilometer   160 miles per hour..257 kilometers per hour

Ron Hornaday (**left**) *won the Driver Championship in 1996 driving a Chevrolet pickup truck owned by Dale Earnhardt* (**right**). *They sure look pleased!*

INDEX

FURTHER READING

Find out more about racing with these helpful books and organizations:

• *NASCAR 50.* 1998

   A history of NASCAR stock car racing

• *Official NASCAR Trivia.* 1998

• NASCAR's Official Site: www.nascar.com

• www.theautochannel.com

   Everything you've wanted to know about cars, trucks and racing.

• www.goracing.com

   Lots of information on all types of racing. The site also posts the results of every race.